Title: "Pest Control for Everyone: A Comprehensive Guide to Treating Homes and Buildings"

Title: "Pest Control for Everyone: A Comprehensive Guide to Treating Homes and Buildings"

I0440362

CHAPTER ONE: INTRODUCTION: UNVEILING THE SECRETS OF PEST CONTROL

- Importance of Pest Control
- Safety and Responsibility

CHAPTER TWO:
UNDERSTANDING PESTS

- Common Household Pests
- Pest Behavior and Habitats

CHAPTER THREE: INSPECTION AND ASSESSMENT- YOUR PEST CONTROL RECON AND   DEFENSE

- How to Inspect for Pests
- Identifying Pest Entry Points

CHAPTER FOUR: PEST PREVENTION- THE DEFENSE STRATEGY

- Maintaining a Clean Environment
- Effective Pest-Proofing Techniques

CHAPTER FIVE: SAFE PEST CONTROL METHODS

- Chemical vs. Non-Chemical Approaches
- Eco-Friendly Options

CHAPTER SIX: CUSTOMER INTERACTIONS

- Building Trust
- Communication Skills

CHAPTER SEVEN: PEST CONTROL ETHICS

- Treating Customers Homes with Respect
- Ethical Considerations in Pest Control

CHAPTER EIGHT: CASE STUDIES AND EXAMPLES

- Real-Life Scenarios and Solutions

CHAPTER NINE:
TROUBLESHOOTING

- Dealing with Challenging Pest Control Situations

CHAPTER TEN: RESOURCES

- Helpful Websites, Books, and Organizations

CHAPTER ELEVEN: CONCLUSION

- The Role of Pest Control in Health and Well-being

Important Note of how I want you to see the pest world: Understanding Pests - The Investigative Approach

In the world of pest control, knowledge is your most potent weapon. Just as a military commander studies their adversaries, understanding pests is our first step towards victory. Welcome to a crash course in the art of investigation as we dive into the world of pests, their behaviors, and their habitats.

CHAPTER ONE: INTRODUCTION: UNVEILING THE SECRETS OF PEST CONTROL

Welcome to the fascinating world of pest control, where science meets the art of safeguarding homes and health. This book is your ticket to a journey that will not only enhance your pest control skills but also deepen your appreciation for the magic of this industry.

The Buzz About Pest Control

You might wonder what all the buzz is about in the world of pest control. Well, we are here to tell you that it's not just about shooing away those pesky intruders. It's about understanding the secret lives of the critters, learning their ways, and mastering the art of evicting them while keeping everyone safe.

Safety: Our Guiding Star

In this adventure, our guiding star is safety. Whether you are a newbie to the industry or a seasoned pro, you will discover that safety is non-negotiable. Think of it as the hero's cape, protecting you, your clients, and the environment from harm's way. It's the cornerstone of everything we do.

Embrace the Responsibility

But here's the secret sauce: Pest control is not just a job; it's a noble responsibility. It's about creating spaces where families can sleep soundly, kitchens can stay bug-free, and gardens can thrive. It's about transforming ordinary spaces into sanctuaries free from the chaos of unwanted guests.

Now, whether you're new to the scene or an old hand, this book will be your trusty sidekick. We've sprinkled it with real-life stories, practical tips, and a dash of humor to keep you engaged. We'll unveil the mysteries of pests and show you the tricks of the trade. Together, we'll journey through an industry that's not only essential but also surprisingly intriguing.

So, fasten your seatbelt, or should we say, your safety gear, and let us explore the enchanting world of pest control. Welcome to an industry that is all about making homes healthier, happier, and dare we say, a little less creepy-crawly. Let's dive in!

CHAPTER TWO:
UNDERSTANDING PESTS

Picture this: just like a seasoned general knows the enemy's infantry, artillery, and cavalry, you should recognize your common household pests. These are the foot soldiers in the pest army, and they come in all shapes and sizes. From the stealthy ants invading your kitchen like a covert operation to the mosquitoes buzzing around your backyard like a relentless airstrike, these pests each have their tactics.

- All crawling pest like Ants & beetles: The infantry of the pest world, they move in organized ranks, exploiting tiny gaps in your defenses.

- All Flying Pest like Wasp & Mosquitoes: The airborne assailants, swooping in under the cover of darkness, ready to launch a sneak attack on your skin.

- All Crawling Pest that likes to infest locations like Cockroaches: The elusive guerrilla fighters, hiding in the shadows, and emerging when you least expect it.

Understanding these common pests is like deciphering the enemy's code. Once you know their tactics and hideouts, you can develop your strategy.

Pest Behavior and Habitats: Spies in the Shadows

Imagine you are a military intelligence officer. To outsmart your adversary, you need to know where they operate and how they behave. Similarly, pests have their strongholds and patterns.

- Bed Bugs: These nocturnal spies prefer dark corners and crevices in your bedroom, coming out at night to feast on blood.

- Rodents: Masters of infiltration, they seek shelter in your walls, attics, and basements, following their supply routes.

- Termites: Silent destroyers, they tunnel through wooden structures, causing hidden damage.

By understanding these pest behaviors and habitats, you can predict their movements, intercept them, and thwart their plans.

In the military, investigation sets the stage for a successful operation. In the world of pest control, understanding pests is your investigative mission. Armed with this knowledge, you'll be better prepared to defend your territory and secure the peace of your home. So, get ready to decode the secrets of common household pests and unveil their hiding spots. Our journey into the world of pest control continues, one strategic move at a time. ---

CHAPTER THREE: INSPECTION AND ASSESSMENT - YOUR PEST CONTROL RECON AND DEFENSE

Welcome to the heart of the operation, where we inspect for pests and identify their entry points. In this chapter, we'll employ a mix of military and civilian strategies, emphasizing the importance of IPM (Integrated Pest Management), and other key tactics to ensure you're well-prepared for the mission.

How to Inspect for Pests: Military Scouting Meets Sherlock Holmes

In the Military: Just as military scouts gather critical information before an operation, you, as a pest control expert, are the scout of your home. Use Integrated Pest Management (IPM) techniques – a comprehensive approach to pest control. Start with a systematic sweep of your territory, surveying for any signs of pest activity.

In Civilian Terms: Think of yourself as a detective. Look for clues like chewed wires, droppings, or damaged items. Examine every nook and cranny, from the kitchen to the garage. Follow the breadcrumbs, or in this case, the droppings, to pinpoint the intruders.

Identifying Pest Entry Points: Fortifying the Perimeter

In the Military: In a military operation, securing entry points is vital. In your pest control mission, implement IPM by preventing pests from entering in the first place. Think of your home as a fortress. Seal off cracks, crevices, and openings – this is the equivalent of fortifying your defenses against a pest invasion.

In Civilian Terms: Imagine your home as a castle. Keep the drawbridge (doors) tightly closed and reinforce your castle walls (walls and windows) to prevent pests from storming the castle. Use caulk, weatherstripping, and screens to block any potential breaches.

Additional Tips: Keep Pests at Bay

Cheman Away Trees from Touching Structures: In your civilian mission, do not forget the strategic importance of landscape management. Just as military clearances must be heavily guarded to prevent ambushes; remember to keep trees and vegetation away from touching your home's structure. This prevents pests from using the branches as a bridge to infiltrate.

1.   Guard the Roof Line: In your home's defense plan, the roof line is critical. Just as military strategists protect key points, safeguard your roof and attic. Use screens, check for any gaps, and ensure proper ventilation. This guards against both flying and crawling infiltrators.

2.   Moisture Control: Finally, control the moisture. Water leaks and drips inside your structure, touching your exterior walls or foundation, create favorable conditions for pests. Just like in the military, denying the enemy a place to hide is a key strategy. Fix leaks promptly and keep the structure dry.

By combining military precision with IPM techniques and additional strategies, you're better equipped to inspect for pests, secure your home, and control the environment that pests find hospitable food, water, and a place to live. Your home is your stronghold, and you're the commander of this pest defense mission.

CHAPTER FOUR: PEST PREVENTION - THE DEFENSE STRATEGY

In this chapter, we'll unveil the essential strategies to prevent pests from infiltrating your territory, whether you're a pest control technician or a homeowner. Think of it as a blend of military precision and everyday civilian know-how.

Maintaining a Clean Environment: The Base Camp Sanitation

In the Military: Just as soldiers maintain a clean and orderly base camp to prevent diseases and pests, your home needs the same level of attention. Sanitation is key, like maintaining cleanliness in a military camp. Eliminate food and water sources - these are your 'supply depots' for pests. Regularly clean and remove debris; it's like keeping the base camp spotless.

In Civilian Terms: For homeowners, picture your home as a fortress, and cleanliness is your shield. Ensure that there are no crumbs, spills, or uncovered food items that can attract pests. Just as soldiers keep their area clean, you must do the same to deter pests.

Effective Pest-Proofing Techniques: Creating Barriers

In the Military: In a military operation, creating barriers is essential to keep the enemy at bay. In pest control, think of pest-proofing your home as building barriers. Seal entry points just as soldiers do with barriers. Block gaps, caulk cracks, and install screens – it's like creating walls to keep pests out. *In Civilian Terms*: In your civilian mission, you are the architect of your home's defenses. Ensure your doors and windows are sealed tightly, like the gates of a castle. Use caulk to plug holes and weatherstripping to create barriers. Install screens on doors and windows – think of them as your protective shields.

Pheromones: The Insect Traffic Lights

Now, let's unveil the secret language of pests. Insects, like tiny traffic controllers, use chemical signals known as pheromones to communicate. It's their way of displaying "Go" and "Stop" signs for their own kind.

- Green Light (Go): Imagine the scent of a freshly baked pie leading you to the kitchen. For pests like ants, they leave a "green light" pheromone trail when they discover food or water. It's like a neon arrow saying, "Follow this path for sustenance!"

- Red Light (Do Not Enter): On the flip side, some pests use a "red light" signal, like a "no entry" sign. Cockroaches, for example, emit pheromones in areas they consider ideal for shelter. It's their way of saying, "This spot is taken; find another place to live."

Steel Wool and Glue Traps: The Entryway Guards and Silent Seekers

In your pest defense strategy, you have two more allies - steel wool and glue traps.

Steel Wool: Think of steel wool as your entryway guard. Just as military sentries protect crucial points, steel wool seals off entryways where pests might sneak in. It's like a strong gate, impervious to their advances.

Glue Traps: Imagine glue traps as silent seekers, much like scouts looking for hidden enemies. Place these traps strategically to discover where pests are lurking in your structures. When they attempt to cross, they become ensnared, revealing their locations.

Sealing Off All Entry Points: The Key to Total Defense

In addition to steel wool and glue traps, remember that pests and rodents can use any opening they can fit their bodies through. Even small gaps, such as those where you can slide a business card, are potential entryways. Rodents can enter through holes as small as a nickel to a quarter. Therefore, it's crucial to seal around pipes, cracks, and crevices, ensuring there are no gaps in your defense.

Pipes and electrical wires inside structures act like highways for pests and rodents to travel within walls, just as military supply routes are vital for troops.
Seal these areas to prevent pest movements inside your domain.
By sealing every potential entry point and pathway for pests and rodents, you're creating a comprehensive defense strategy. Your home or establishment becomes an impenetrable fortress, allowing pests no chance of infiltration. This multi-layered approach ensures that you're not only keeping the doors closed to pests but also sealing off all other hidden routes they might exploit.

CHAPTER FIVE: SAFE PEST CONTROL METHODS

In this chapter, we'll explore the world of pest control technicians and their methods for keeping both customers and the environment safe while dealing with pests. These techniques are like strategies in both civilian and military contexts, and they range from wielding various "weapons," including chemical treatments, to employing eco-friendly tactics.

Continuous Education: The Military Training

Just as soldiers undergo continuous training to stay sharp, pest control technicians continuously educate themselves and earn certifications in House Pest Control (HPC) and Wood Destroying Organisms (WDO) to be well-equipped to tackle various pest-related challenges.

Creating Long-Lasting Barriers: Implementing Defensive Measures

Picture a military strategy to safeguard a territory. Pest control technicians implement defensive measures around your home using liquid treatments, not just for short-term results but for long-lasting control, determined to keep enemy forces at bay for up to 90 days. These modern chemicals are the advanced weapons, designed for effectiveness and safety.

The First Step: Reading the Orders

In military operations, reading the orders is crucial. In pest control, technicians start by reading product labels, ensuring safe and effective deployment. This is like studying the battle plan, maintaining a balance between pest control and environmental safety.

Regular Rotations for Pest and Rodent Management: Patrols and Reinforcements

Significant to military patrols, pest control requires routine rotations. Typically, treatments should be rescheduled every 30 to 90 days. For heavy infestations, think of it as sending reinforcements every two weeks. Bait is your tactical weapon against ants and German roaches. It often contains Insect Growth Regulators (IGR) to disrupt the enemy's development and reproduction.

Slow Killers with Long-Lasting Impact: The Silent Assassins

Modern pest control chemicals are like silent assassins. When pest encounters the chemicals, their nervous systems are affected within 10 to 15 minutes. It is a slow but effective kill, different from the quick-action chemicals you find at local convenience stores.

The Power of Dust: A Strategic Move

Imagine using a strategic move to weaken the enemy. In pest control, dust is your weapon. It dries up the exoskeleton of insects, leading to their dehydration and ultimate demise. It is the chemical affecting their ranks, much like a tactical approach.

The Microscopic beads Covert Agents

Some pest control technicians employ microscopic agents, like secret agents. These agents, known as CS products, attach to the enemy's body, perfect for taking down specific targets like spiders and other contact insects.

Trophallaxis: Eliminating Leadership

In military terms, it is like taking down the enemy's leadership. In social insects, Trophallaxis, or mouth-feeding, is vital. Pest control technicians aim to eliminate not just the soldiers but the base of the enemy - the queen, the king, and the queen. This is the key to victory, much like targeting the enemy's command structure.

Chemical vs. Non-Chemical Approaches: Choosing Your Weapons

The pest control industry offers a variety of approaches, much like choosing the right weapons for a mission. Technicians use their knowledge and expertise to select the most suitable method for each unique pest challenge, considering both safety and effectiveness.

Fumigation: Evacuation Required

In certain cases, fumigation products act like a potent bomb, but it requires evacuation, much like civilians leaving their homes during military operations. This ensures the safety of occupants and their return to a pest-free and secure environment.

By exploring these safe and innovative pest control methods, you gain insight into the industry's commitment to protecting both your home and the environment while effectively managing pests. It is a harmonious balance between science, technology, and eco-consciousness, ensuring that the battle against pests is won without compromising safety and sustainability, much like a military campaign that secures the homeland without collateral damage.

CHAPTER SIX: CUSTOMER INTERACTIONS

In this chapter, let us journey into the art of customer interactions in the pest control industry, drawing inspiration from both military and civilian tactics. We will explore the fundamental elements of building trust, honing effective communication skills, and the importance of post-service follow-up. Highlighting the principle of treating every home as if it were your own and emphasize the significance of ongoing communication.

Building Trust: The Bedrock of Success

In the Military: Trust is the glue that holds military units together. Just as soldiers rely on one another on the battlefield, in pest control, building trust with your customers is the bedrock of success. They must have faith that you will oversee their pest-related challenges with utmost professionalism.

In Civilian Terms: Imagine your customer's home as an extension of your own. Just as you meticulously care for your personal space, treating your customer's home as if it were your own is a powerful way to build trust. It signifies a commitment to their well-being and safety.

Communication Skills: The Bridge of Understanding

In the Military: On the front lines, communication is the bridge that ensures everyone is on the same page and working towards a common goal. In the pest control industry, your communication skills must be fine-tuned to convey the steps and expectations clearly to your customers.

In Civilian Terms: When discussing the pest control process, employ clear and straightforward language. Think of it as giving precise orders to your team, ensuring every detail is understood. Be ready to answer questions, address concerns, and provide guidance, keeping the customer well-informed at every step.

Follow-up: The Assurance of Continued Care

In both military and civilian contexts, follow-up is an essential practice. After providing pest control services, reaching out to your customers at the two-week mark is a proactive way to ensure their situation is under control. It's like a check-in after a mission to confirm that the plan is working. This communication is key to maintaining a strong relationship and assuring your customers that their well-being remains a top priority.

Remember the golden rule: "I was taught to always treat every home like it's my own. If you take care of yours, you will take care of others." This principle, rooted in respect and responsibility, transcends both military and civilian spheres. It underscores the significance of respecting and nurturing the environments and properties of those you serve.

By mastering the art of customer interactions and including regular follow-up, you not only ensure the success of your pest control mission but also cultivate lasting relationships with your customers. Just as military units rely on cohesion and effective communication, you and your customers collaborate to protect their homes from pests with the utmost care and professionalism.

CHAPTER SEVEN: PEST CONTROL ETHICS

In this chapter, we will delve into the world of pest control integrity, which is as vital as any strategy in the industry. We'll focus on the fundamental principle of treating customers' homes with respect and cover various important considerations that pest control pros should be aware of in their work. Let's stress the importance of maintaining high standards of integrity, ensuring a safe and cooperative relationship between pest control technicians and their customers.

Treating Customers' Homes with Respect: A Pest Control Fundamental

In the Pest Control Industry: The core of maintaining integrity in pest control is the respectful treatment of customers' homes. Just as soldiers respect the territory they are in; pest control pros must respect the homes they serve. This respect extends to the property, privacy, and overall well-being of the customers.

Important Considerations in Pest Control: Upholding Standards

Pest control integrity is about more than just doing the job. It's about ensuring a safe and cooperative working relationship between pest control technicians and their customers. Here are some important considerations that every pest control pro should follow:

- No Theft: Just as a commander expects honesty in the ranks, pest control pros should never steal from their customers. Honesty is paramount.

- No Harassment: Unwanted advances or comments have no place in pest control. Pest control technicians should always maintain professionalism and respect.

- Sober and Alert: Working under the influence of drugs or alcohol is a big no. Pest control professionals should always be sober and alert to ensure safety.

- Truthful Representation: Honesty should be the rule in all interactions with customers. Misleading customers or lying to make a sale is unacceptable and breaks trust.

- Safety First: Be careful to avoid physical and mental burnout that can exhaust you to the point where you are not able to perform your job properly. Ensure you are in the right mindset and think before you act. Driving is especially critical in this industry, so prioritize safety, safety, safety.

- Environmental Responsibility: Pest control integrity also includes environmental responsibility. Use eco-friendly methods whenever possible and minimize harm to non-target species. Protect pollinators like bees by avoiding harmful products that may harm these important species and the protective rodents in your state.

By following these important considerations, pest control pros ensure that they not only get rid of pests effectively but also maintain the trust and respect of their customers. Pest control integrity is about delivering a valuable service while upholding the highest standards of honesty, safety, and environmental responsibility. This creates a win-win situation for both the industry and its customers commercial or residential.

CHAPTER EIGHT: CASE STUDIES AND EXAMPLES

Scenario: The Nighttime Crawl

Wesley Lowery, the owner of W.L PEST Control LLC in Grayson, Georgia, began his pest control journey in 2014. His path in the industry took him from the streets of Grayson to a memorable job in a crawlspace. He was with Terminix
International out of Summerville, South Carolina at the time, conducting a termite inspection. As he crawled on top of a vapor barrier in the dark, with just a headlamp to light his way, the unexpected happened.

The situation was anything but ordinary. Wesley was crawling in cramped spaces, sometimes with just 18 inches or less of clearance. In one such scenario, he felt a vibration, believing it was his phone in his crawl suit. As he unzipped his suit to check, he realized that it was not his phone vibrating. He looked down and found himself face-to-face with a possum trapped under a snake, squealing for its life.

In that moment, panic and adrenaline took over. He yelled and screamed for his trainer, all the while knowing that the homeowners were upstairs, unaware of the drama unfolding beneath their house, which was already under stress from a termite infestation they were inspecting.

His trainer reacted swiftly, pulling out a pick hammer and bashing the snake and the possum. Both Wesley and his trainer hurriedly crawled out from under the vapor barrier, the possum wobbling out behind them. In a brave move, the trainer grabbed the possum by the tail, swung it around in circles, and threw it over the fence. "Okay, I think we got both of them," he said.
As Wesley watched in disbelief, his trainer added, "Now, let's go finish inspecting this house," and went back into the crawlspace. The intensity of the situation was etched in Wesley's mind, and he knew without delay that this was a job like no other, one that would test his courage and determination.

But that was just day one. Wesley's journey in pest control became filled with heart- pounding moments. On another occasion, he found himself standing on top of a fire ant mound at a church facing a busy intersection, only to discover that fire ants had climbed up his legs. Stripping down to escape the stinging pests became a spontaneous street-side performance.

On his third day, while knocking down spiderwebs, a 12-foot lizard leaped off a rooftop and into his crawl suit, setting the stage for an impromptu dance performance that impressed both the home's two barking dogs and the astonished onlookers.

And then there was the comprehensive termite treatment under a house built in the 1800s. There, he bumped into a paper wasp nest and had a heart-pounding encounter with his biggest fear: a nest full of cellar spiders. They crawled all over his body inside his crawl suit, and he did not realize it until it was already too late. It was another day that ended with an unexpected strip show.

This scenario is a testament to the unexpected challenges and thrilling experiences that await those who choose a career in pest control. It's a reminder that pest control professionals need to be prepared for anything, from impromptu dances to unexpected encounters with stinging and crawling creatures. It's an adventure-filled career that requires not only bravery but a good sense of humor.

Whether you're a pest control professional or a homeowner tackling pest issues on your own, always be aware of your surroundings. Wesley's experiences highlight the importance of staying vigilant and prepared, as you may find yourself in unique and thrilling situations that require quick thinking and a good sense of humor. Every day in the world of pest control is an adventure, filled with opportunities to gain experience, adapt, and make a difference.

CHAPTER 9: TROUBLESHOOTING - DEALING WITH CHALLENGING PEST CONTROL SITUATIONS

In this chapter, we delve into the complexities of dealing with challenging pest control situations, while providing valuable insights and solutions.

Military vs. Civilian Precision

In the world of pest control, precision is paramount. Just as the military depends on specialized equipment for specific tasks, pest control technicians must ensure. their gear is tailored to the pests they are up against. Moreover, being mindful of your surroundings is essential.

Pest Control Around Your Home

Here is an essential piece of knowledge for homeowners: If you have trees or bushes touching your structure, chances are you may have rodents finding their way into your attic. These unwelcome visitors often gain access to your attic from the gutter line. Many pest control companies may propose exclusion jobs to remedy this problem, which can be quite expensive. However, a simpler solution is to trim away tree branches and relocate bushes, creating a less hospitable environment for rodents.

Now, let's discuss one of the often-overlooked habits of rodents. Just like dogs and cats, rodents pee and poop to mark their territory. This territorial marking can lead to new rodents coming into your home, even if some of them have died. Key areas to check include inside the hot water heater closet, behind appliances like the stove, refrigerator, and dishwasher. In locations with extensive storage, rearrange items to prevent rodents from nesting. Basements, storage rooms, attics, and spaces under sinks are popular undisturbed territories where pests and rodents establish comfortable living.

Securing Entryways

Another aspect to consider is closed-off entryways. Rodents and pests frequently exploit gaps beneath garage doors, around doors, and next to the dishwasher. They also favor areas where pipes enter your home. To address these entry points, consider using door strips, and seal off any gaps around pipes, cutting off their preferred routes.

Understanding the Role of Water

Water is vital for both humans and pests. Pest control technicians often compare a structure with unwanted pests to a desert. Just like humans require food, water, and shelter, pests and rodents are no different. When you eliminate their access to these resources, they must either die off or search for new territories. This perspective is essential for pest control. You may have an external AC unit that occasionally drips water, offering a potential water source for pests and rodents. It is imperative to address such water sources to help prevent infestations.

German Roaches: A Particular Challenge

It is important to note that German roaches, which originated in Southeast Asia, are drawn to specific items. Spices in your cabinet can be particularly attractive to them. To control German roaches effectively, store all food items in plastic containers and remove any cardboard boxes. Additionally, they have an affinity for pet food, so be sure to keep it sealed in containers to prevent any unwelcome visitors.

Understanding Pest Behavior

Pests and rodents have intriguing behavior patterns. In the fall, they tend to head to the attic because heat rises, and they can stay warm within the insulation. Conversely, in the heat, they seek refuge in the basement to stay cool.

Effective Pest Control Methods

To keep your property free of rodents, consider using rodent stations outside your structure. These stations act like drive-through restaurants for rodents. Additionally, rodent bait is a highly effective way to control them, and its tamper- proof. Furthermore, you can employ dust and baits for dealing with roaches. Equip yourself with a duster for applying dust and a bait gun for roach and ant bait. Bait stations are a reliable choice for controlling pests like roaches and ants.

As you navigate the intricacies of pest control, understanding the nuances of pest behavior and adopting the appropriate techniques are vital for success. By following these strategies, you can maintain a pest-free home, ensuring a safer and more comfortable living environment.

CHAPTER 10: RESOURCES - HELPFUL WEBSITES, BOOKS, AND ORGANIZATIONS

In this final chapter, we present a collection of valuable resources, both online and offline, that will further enhance your understanding of pest control and provide you with the tools and knowledge needed to navigate this field effectively.

Books and Publications

While the internet provides a wealth of information, books and publications remain valuable sources of in-depth knowledge. Here are a few must-reads for anyone serious about pest control:

- "The Mallis Handbook of Pest Control" by Arnold Mallis: A comprehensive guide for pest management professionals, this book covers a wide range of pests and control methods.

- "Urban Pest Management: An Environmental Perspective" by Partho Dhang: This book explores urban pest management from an environmental standpoint, making it a valuable resource for eco-conscious pest control.

- "Pest Control Technology Magazine": Stay informed with this leading industry magazine. It offers articles, reviews, and updates on pest control trends and technologies.
- "Cockroach Combat 2" by Dr. Austin M. Frishman and Paul J. Bello: This book offers in-depth insights into combating cockroaches and is a valuable resource for those dealing with these persistent pests.

Local Pest Control Companies

Often, your local pest control companies maintain informative websites. These websites can offer insights into regional pest issues, services offered, and contact details. Consider visiting the website of a pest control company in your area, as it can be a valuable resource for understanding the specific challenges you might face locally.

Connect with Pest Control Professionals

One of the most valuable resources is connecting with experienced pest control professionals. If you are facing a specific pest issue or have questions about pest control methods, don't hesitate to reach out to a local pest control expert. They can provide tailored guidance and solutions.

W.L PEST Control LLC:
  - Website: www.wlpest.com
  - Instagram: [@wlpestcontrollc](https://www.instagram.com/wlpestcontrollc/)

- Facebook: [W.L PEST Control LLC on Facebook](https://www.facebook.com/ wlpestcontrollc)
- YouTube: [W.L PEST Control LLC on YouTube](https://www.youtube.com/c/ WLPESTControlLLC)

By utilizing these resources, you will have a solid foundation to build your expertise and effectively manage pest-related challenges. Learning is an ongoing process in the field of pest control, and these resources will be instrumental in your journey.

CHAPTER 11: CONCLUSION - THE ROLE OF PEST CONTROL IN HEALTH AND WELL-BEING

As we draw the curtain on our exploration of the world of pest control, we uncover a profound understanding of its role in safeguarding health and well-being. Pests, from the persistent German roaches to the notorious bedbugs, invasive ants, and even venomous spiders, present challenges far beyond mere annoyances. They pose tangible threats to our physical and mental health.

The Threats Pests Bring

- German Roaches: These resilient insects infiltrate our homes and businesses, contaminating our environments and tainting our food sources. Their presence can be connected to allergies, asthma, and even foodborne illnesses, underscoring their significance.
- Bedbugs: Beyond causing discomfort, these elusive creatures disrupt our sleep and introduce us to the world of skin irritations.

- Ants: Though not intrinsically hazardous, ants serve as vectors, bringing harmful bacteria into our living spaces, putting our health at risk.

- Spiders: The specter of venomous bites looms with spiders like the brown recluse and black widow, inviting the threat of severe health repercussions if left unchecked.

- Fleas and Ticks: Carriers of disease, these bloodsuckers pose health risks to both us and our beloved pets.

- Rodents: Mice and rats, known carriers of diseases, navigate our homes and put our food and well-being in peril.

Health and Hygiene

The impact of pests is not isolated; it reverberates throughout our communities, introducing threats of food contamination and disease transmission. Consider the broader implications of pest control:

- Food Safety: The hospitality industry grapples with the constant threat of foodborne diseases due to contamination. Pest control is the linchpin in these establishments' prevention strategies.

- Sanitation Challenges: Pests and rodents thrive in unsanitary environments, compelling the importance of pest control in maintaining hygiene standards, whether in homes or businesses.

- PPE (Personal Protective Equipment): Pest control professionals understand the paramount importance of Personal Protective Equipment. The correct use of protective gear ensures safety when engaging with these health-sensitive scenarios.

A Collective Pursuit of Health and Well-being

Much like in military endeavors and civilian life, collaboration stands at the forefront. In the realm of pest control, this collaboration is instrumental. Here's how customers and providers combine forces to wield influence:

- Customers: Upholding clean and sanitary living or working spaces is not just a responsibility but a commitment. Regular maintenance, proper food storage, and prompt reporting of pest issues all fall within the purview of customers.

- Providers: Pest control professionals bring a wealth of knowledge to the table. Their mastery of pests, skilled utilization of pesticides, and keen recognition of the integral role of sanitation are instrumental in health preservation.

Through this combined effort, customers and providers champion health and well-being by guarding against the menaces posed by pests and rodents. Pest- free environments are the cornerstone of healthier lives and bolstered safety.
This collaboration mirrors the significance of security in both military and civilian domains.

In conclusion, remember that pest control is not merely a service; it is a guardian of health and well-being. The battle against pests may be relentless, but it's a battle of profound importance. It's a testament to our unwavering dedication to crafting healthier and safer living environments for ourselves, our cherished ones, and our entire communities. It's a commitment to well-being, a sentinel of health, and a promise for a safer, pest-free future.

NOTES

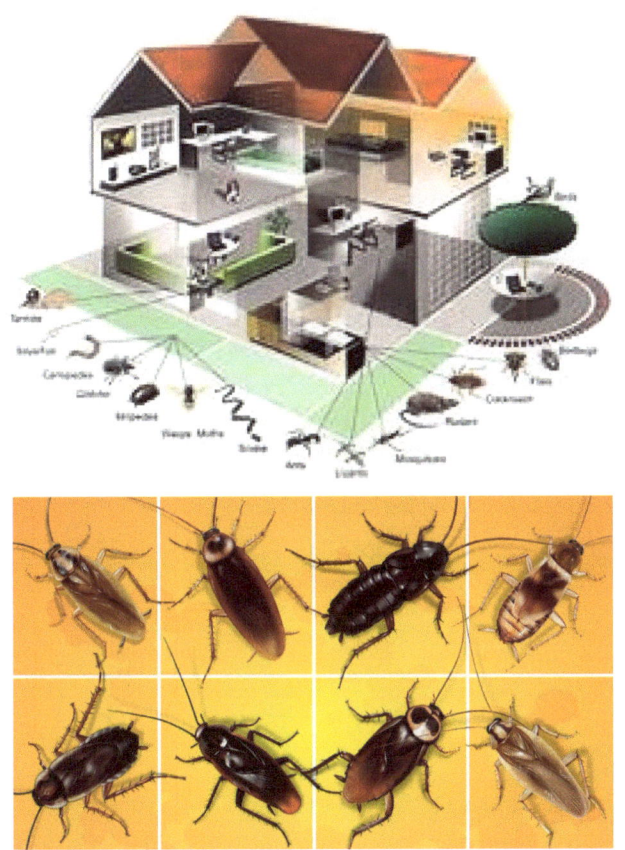

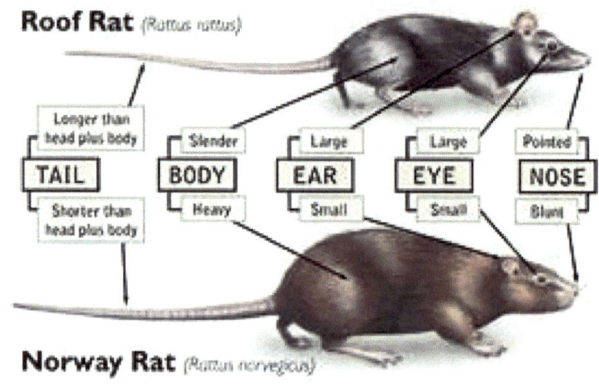